Eye-catching argyle patterns have taken the crochet world by storm, causing amazement when people learn that the patterns appear like magic from the color variations in popular yarns. A pioneer in discovering the secrets of planned color pooling for crochet, Marly Bird has written this simple guide book for using the technique in scarves, a poncho, and other easy projects. For greater understanding, she recommends viewing her tutorial videos at http://www.marlybird.com/category/planned-pooling/.

LEISURE ARTS, INC. • Maumelle, Arkansas

Planned Yarn Pooling

1. It is highly recommended that you watch Marly Bird's tutorial videos on planned color pooling to better understand how the body is made: http://bit.ly/2hoslgr_CrochetPlannedPoolingPlaylist
2. You may have to tighten or loosen some stitches as you go in order to keep the color pooling intact. Keep a variety of hook sizes on hand to help resize your stitches.
3. Different dye lots of the same colorway may change the number of stitches obtained in any given color. Count the number of stitches YOU get to work through one full color sequence, as well as in each color section, and maintain that throughout the pattern.

Meet Marly Bird

Marly Bird fled the world of financial services to launch a career in the yarn industry, and she hasn't looked back since. To Marly, a bi-crafty girl who both knits and crochets, the yarn is the star, not how you work with it.

She is the national spokesperson for Red Heart Yarns, hosts the YarnThing podcast, and has had designs published in numerous Leisure Arts books, including I Can't Believe I'm Entrelac Knitting (see leisurearts.com). Marly also is author of Cold Weather Crochet and co-author of Knitting for Dummies, 3rd ed. You've seen her designs in Knitter's Magazine, Interweave Crochet, Knitscene, Love of Crochet, Love of Knitting, and in books on socks, afghans, lace, sweaters, and more.

Marly has a successful YouTube channel where she teaches both knitting and crochet. She also has online classes with Creativebug and Craftsy.com. For more about Marly, visit marlybird.com.

Full Scarf

EASY

Finished Size: 10" x 80" (25.5 cm x 203 cm)

SHOPPING LIST

Yarn (Medium Weight)

MEDIUM 4

[5 ounces, 236 yards
(141 grams, 215 meters) per skein]:

☐ 2 skeins

Crochet Hook

☐ Size J (6 mm)
or size needed for gauge

Extra hooks in neighboring sizes
(see Planned Yarn Pooling, page 2)

Additional Supplies

☐ Yarn needle

GAUGE INFORMATION

In Moss St, 13 sts (sc and chs) and 13 rows = 4" (10 cm)

Gauge Swatch: 4" (10 cm) square

Ch 14.

Row 1: Skip 3 ch **(counts as a st)**, sc in next ch, ★ ch 1, skip 1 foundation ch, sc in next ch; repeat from ★ to end.

Row 2: Ch 2 **(counts as a st, now and throughout)**, turn; sc in next ch-1 sp, ★ ch 1, sc in next ch-1 sp; repeat from ★ to end finishing with a sc in last ch-3 sp.

Rows 3-13: Ch 2, turn; sc in next ch-1 sp, ★ ch 1, sc in next ch-1 sp; repeat from ★ to end finishing with a sc in last ch-2 sp. Finish off.

STITCH GUIDE

MOSS STITCH *(abbreviated Moss St)*

Ch an even number of sts.

Row 1: Skip 3 ch **(counts as a st)**, sc in next ch, ★ ch 1, skip 1 foundation ch, sc in next ch; repeat from ★ to end.

Row 2: Ch 2 **(counts as a st, now and throughout)**, turn; sc in next ch-1 sp, ★ ch 1, sc in next ch-1 sp; repeat from ★ to end finishing with a sc in last ch-3 sp.

Row 3: Ch 2, turn; sc in next ch-1 sp, ★ ch 1, sc in next ch-1 sp; repeat from ★ to end finishing with a sc in last ch-2 sp.

Repeat Row 3 for Moss St.

SCARF

With A, ch through at least 1 full color sequence, with the last loop on hook being the first loop of a new color just after a color change in the yarn.

Row 1 (Right side): Skip 3 ch **(counts as a st)**, sc in 4th ch from hook, ★ ch 1, sc around the foundation ch (instead of going into a ch st); repeat from ★ until 1 full color sequence has been completed. Count the number of sc made in each individual color in the colorway and note it down. Leave remaining ch sts unworked. Undo one st repeat (sc, ch 1).

Note: Loop a short piece of yarn around any stitch to mark Row 1 as **right** side.

Row 2: Ch 2 **(counts as a st, now and throughout)**, turn; sc in next ch-1 sp, ★ ch 1, sc in next ch-1 sp; repeat from ★ to end finishing with a sc in last ch-3 sp.

Note: As you work this row and all remaining rows, you MUST get the correct number of sc in each color in order to maintain the planned color pooling. Change hook sizes, or actual st used, to get the correct color in place. If you use the same number of sts per color that you counted on Row 1, it will work out.

Row 3: Ch 2, turn; sc in next ch-1 sp, ★ ch 1, sc in the next ch-1 sp; repeat from ★ to end, finishing with a sc in last ch-2 sp.

Note: The color of the sts on this row will shift to the left or right by 1st from the previous right side row depending on the colorway and if you are right or left handed. It doesn't matter which direction the stitch shifts as long as it is off-set by 1.

Row 4: Ch 2, turn; sc in next ch-1 sp, ★ ch 1, sc in the next ch-1 sp; repeat from ★ to end, finishing with a sc in last ch-2 sp.

Note: The color of the sts on this row will shift to the left or right by 1 st from the previous wrong side row depending on the colorway and if you are right or left handed. It doesn't matter which direction the stitch shifts as long as it is off-set by 1.

Repeat Rows 3 and 4 until piece measures 80" (203 cm) ending on a Row 3 (right side row).

Finish off.

FINISHING

Squish or stretch the sts on foundation chain to match the width of the rest of the scarf. You can slide the sts around along the foundation chain, as with an adjustable ring. Unravel unused foundation ch sts and weave in yarn tail to secure foundation.

EDGING

Rnd 1: With **right** side facing and working across foundation edge, join with slip st in foundation ch st under last sc of Row 1; ch 2, sc once more in same ch, ★ ch 1, sc in next sp between sc of Row 1; repeat from ★ to ch-3 corner sp, (ch 1, sc) 3 times in corner sp, rotate Scarf to work along long side edge, (ch 1, sc) in each ch sp at edge of every other row to corner sc, (ch 1, sc) twice around corner sc, rotate Scarf to work along top edge, (ch 1, sc) in each ch-1 sp to corner ch-2 sp, (ch 1, sc) 3 times in corner sp, rotate Scarf to work along long side edge, (ch 1, sc) in each ch sp at edge of every other row to corner sc, (ch 1, sc) twice around corner sc, ch 1; join with slip st in beginning ch-2, finish off.

Weave in all loose ends.

Wristers, Cowl, & Hat Set

EASY

Finished Size:
Wristlets - 8" x 8" (20.5 cm x 20.5 cm)
Hat - 8" x 22" (20.5 cm x 56 cm)
Cowl - 8" x 30" (20.5 cm x 76 cm)
All measurements given with pieces laid flat, before assembly.

SHOPPING LIST

Yarn (Medium Weight) MEDIUM 4

[5 ounces, 236 yards
(141 grams, 215 meters) per skein]:
- ☐ Variegated - 2 skeins

[7 ounces 364 yards
(198 grams, 333 meters) per skein]:
- ☐ Grey - 1 skein

Crochet Hook

- ☐ Size J (6 mm)
  or size needed for gauge

Extra hooks in neighboring sizes
(see Planned Yarn Pooling, page 2)

Additional Supplies

- ☐ Pom-pom maker, 1½" (4 cm) diameter
- ☐ 1" (2.5 cm) decorative buttons - 3
- ☐ Yarn needle

GAUGE INFORMATION

In Moss St, 13 sts (sc and chs) and 13 rows = 4" (10 cm)
Gauge Swatch: 4" (10 cm) square
Ch 14.
Row 1: Skip 3 ch **(counts as a st)**, sc in next ch, ★ ch 1, skip 1 foundation ch, sc in next ch; repeat from ★ to end.
Row 2: Ch 2 **(counts as a st, now and throughout)**, turn; sc in next ch-1 sp, ★ ch 1, sc in next ch-1 sp; repeat from ★ to end finishing with a sc in last ch-3 sp.
Rows 3-13: Ch 2, turn; sc in next ch-1 sp, ★ ch 1, sc in next ch-1 sp; repeat from ★ to end finishing with a sc in last ch-2 sp.
Finish off.

STITCH GUIDE

MOSS STITCH *(abbreviated Moss St)*
Ch an even number of sts.
Row 1: Skip 3 ch **(counts as a st)**, sc in next ch, ★ ch 1, skip 1 foundation ch, sc in next ch; repeat from ★ to end, turn.
Row 2: Ch 2 **(counts as a st, now and throughout)**, turn; sc in next ch-1 sp, ★ ch 1, sc in next ch-1 sp; repeat from ★ to end finishing with a sc in last ch-3 sp.
Row 3: Ch 2, turn; sc in next ch-1 sp, ★ ch 1, sc in next ch-1 sp; repeat from ★ to end finishing with a sc in last ch-2 sp.
Repeat Row 3 for Moss St.

WRISTLET (Make 2)

With Variegated, ch through at least 1 full color sequence, with the last loop on hook being the first loop of a new color just after a color change in the yarn.

Row 1 (Right side)**:** Skip 3 ch **(counts as a st)**, sc in the 4th ch from hook, ★ ch 1, sc around the foundation ch (instead of going into a ch st); repeat from ★ until 1 full color sequence has been completed. Count the number of sc made in each individual color in the colorway and note it down. Leave remaining ch sts unworked. Undo one st repeat (sc, ch 1).

Note: Loop a short piece of yarn around any stitch to mark Row 1 as **right** side.

Row 2: Ch 2 **(counts as a st, now and throughout)**, turn; sc in next ch-1 sp, ★ ch 1, sc in next ch-1 sp; repeat from ★ to end finishing with a sc in last ch-3 sp.

Note: As you work this row and all remaining rows, you MUST get the correct number of sc in each color in order to maintain the planned color pooling. Change hook sizes, or actual st used, to get the correct color in place. If you use the same number of sts per color that you counted on Row 1, it will work out.

Row 3: Ch 2, turn; sc in next ch-1 sp, ★ ch 1, sc in the next ch-1 sp; repeat from ★ to end, finishing with a sc in last ch-2 sp.

Note: The color of the sts on this row will shift to the left or right by 1 st from the previous right side row depending on the colorway and if you are right or left handed. It doesn't matter which direction the stitch shifts as long as it is off-set by 1.

Row 4: Ch 2, turn; sc in next ch-1 sp, ★ ch 1, sc in the next ch-1 sp; repeat from ★ to end, finishing with a sc in last ch-2 sp.

Note: The color of the sts on this row will shift to the left or right by 1 st from the previous wrong side row depending on the colorway and if you are right or left handed. It doesn't matter which direction the stitch shifts as long as it is off-set by 1.

Repeat Rows 3 and 4 until piece measures 8" (20.5 cm) ending on a Row 3 (right side row).

Finish off.

FINISHING

Squish or stretch the sts on foundation chain to match the width of the rest of the piece. You can slide the sts around along the foundation chain, as with an adjustable ring. Unravel unused foundation ch sts and weave in yarn tail to secure foundation.

FOUNDATION EDGE:

With **wrong** side facing and working across the foundation chain edge, join Variegated with slip st in ch-3 edge sp, ch 1, sc in same sp, ★ ch 1, sc in next sp between sc of Row 1; repeat from ★ to end of foundation edge, ch 1, slip st in foundation ch st under last sc of Row 1.

Finish off.

EDGING

Row 1: With **wrong** facing and working across one side edge, join Grey with slip st in corner ch-2 sp, ch 2, sc in next edge sp, ★ ch 1, sc in next edge sp; repeat from ★ to end of this edge.

Row 2: Ch 2, turn; sc in next sp, ★ ch 1, sc in next sp; repeat from ★ to end.

Repeat Row 2 once **more**.

Finish off.

Work other side edge the same way.

ASSEMBLY
Sew together top and bottom edges of each piece.

Weave in all loose ends.

HAT
Work Body of Hat same as Wristlets, except continue until piece measures 22" (56 cm).

FINISHING
Work foundation edge same as Wristlets.

EDGING
Work same as Wristlet edging along just one side edge of Hat.

ASSEMBLY
Sew together top and bottom edges of piece.

Fold in half and sew together the top edge opposite the edging, giving the Hat a square construction.

With Grey, make 2 pom-poms and sew one to each corner of Hat.

Weave in all loose ends.

COWL
Work Body of Cowl same as Wristlets, except continue until piece measures 30" (76 cm).

FINISHING
Work foundation edge same as Wristlets.

EDGING
Row 1: With **wrong** facing and working across one side edge, join Grey with slip st in ch-2 corner sp, ch 2, sc in next edge sp, ★ ch 1, sc in next edge sp; repeat from ★ to end of this edge.

Row 2: Ch 2, turn; sc in next sp, ★ ch 1, sc in next sp; repeat from ★ to end, do **not** turn.

Row 3: Ch 2, working from **left** to **right**, reverse sc in next sp ***(Figs. 2a-d, page 31)***, ★ ch 1, reverse sc in next sp; repeat from ★ across.

Finish off.

Work other side edge the same way.

ASSEMBLY
Sew together top and bottom edges of piece.

Weave in all loose ends.

Zig-Zag Scarf

EASY

Finished Size: 4½" x 68" (11.5 cm x 172.5 cm)

SHOPPING LIST

Yarn (Medium Weight)

MEDIUM 4

[5 ounces, 236 yards
(141 grams, 215 meters) per skein]:

- ☐ Variegated - 1 skein

[7 ounces 364 yards
(198 grams, 333 meters) per skein]:

- ☐ Black - 1 skein

Crochet Hook

- ☐ Size J (6 mm)
  or size needed for gauge

Extra hooks in neighboring sizes
(see Planned Yarn Pooling, page 2)

Additional Supplies

- ☐ Yarn needle

GAUGE INFORMATION

In Moss St, 13 sts (sc and chs) and 13 rows = 4" (10 cm)

Gauge Swatch: 4" (10 cm) square

Ch 14.

Row 1: Skip 3 ch **(counts as a st)**, sc in next ch, ★ ch 1, skip 1 foundation ch, sc in next ch; repeat from ★ to end.

Row 2: Ch 2 **(counts as a st, now and throughout)**, turn; sc in next ch-1 sp, ★ ch 1, sc in next ch-1 sp; repeat from ★ to end finishing with a sc in last ch-3 sp.

Rows 3-13: Ch 2, turn; sc in next ch-1 sp, ★ ch 1, sc in next ch-1 sp; repeat from ★ to end finishing with a sc in last ch-2 sp.

Finish off.

STITCH GUIDE

MOSS STITCH ***(abbreviated Moss St)***

Ch an even number of sts.

Row 1: Skip 3 ch **(counts as a st)**, sc in next ch, ★ ch 1, skip 1 foundation ch, sc in next ch; repeat from ★ to end, turn.

Row 2: Ch 2 **(counts as a st, now and throughout)**, turn; sc in next ch-1 sp, ★ ch 1, sc in next ch-1 sp; repeat from ★ to end finishing with a sc in last ch-3 sp.

Row 3: Ch 2, turn; sc in next ch-1 sp, ★ ch 1, sc in next ch-1 sp; repeat from ★ to end finishing with a sc in last ch-2 sp.

Repeat Row 3 for Moss St.

SCARF

With Variegated, ch through one full color sequence, with the last loop on hook being the first loop of a new color just after a color change in the yarn.

Row 1 (Right side)**:** Skip 3 ch **(counts as stitch)**, sc in 4th ch from hook, ★ ch 1, sc around the foundation ch (instead of going into a ch st); repeat from ★ until 1 full color sequence has been completed on this row. Count the number of sc made in each color.

Add the total number of sc on Row 1, divide by 2, round to the even number. Pull out the stitches until only the even number of stitches remain, leave the remaining chains unworked.

Note: Loop a short piece of yarn around any stitch to mark Row 1 as **right** side.

Row 2: Ch 2 **(counts as a st, now and throughout)**, turn; sc in next ch-1 sp, ★ ch 1, sc in next ch-1 sp; repeat from ★ to end finishing with a sc in last ch-3 sp.

Note: As you work this row and all remaining rows, you MUST get the same number of sc in the color st as you did in Row 1 before pulling them out. This is needed to maintain the planned color pooling. Change hook sizes, or actual st used, to get the correct color in place. The half color sequence makes it so you use the same number of sts per color over the course of 2 rows that you counted on Row 1 (remember that the turning chain counts as a stitch).

Row 3: Ch 2 , turn; sc in next ch-1 sp, ★ ch 1, sc in the next ch-1 sp; repeat from ★ to end, finishing with a sc in last ch-2 sp.

Note: The color of the sts on this row will shift to the left or right by 1 st from the previous right side depending on the colorway and if you are right or left handed. It doesn't matter which direction the stitch shifts as long as it is off set by 1.

Row 4: Ch 2, turn; sc in next ch-1 sp, ★ ch 1, sc in the next ch-1 sp; repeat from ★ to end, finishing with a sc in last ch-2 sp.

Note: The color of the sts on this row will shift to the left or right by 1 st from the previous wrong side depending on the colorway and if you are right or left handed. It doesn't matter which direction the stitch shifts as long as it is off set by 1.

Repeat Rows 3 and 4 until Scarf measures 68" (172.5 cm) **or** to desired length.

FINISHING

Squish or stretch the sts on foundation chain to match the width of the rest of the scarf. You can slide the sts around along the foundation chain, as with an adjustable ring.

EDGING

Rnd 1: With **right** side facing and working across the foundation chain edge, join Black with a slip st in foundation chain next to last sc of Row 1, ch 2, (sc, ch 1) once more in ch, sc in next sp between sc of Row 1, ★ ch 1, sc in next sp between sc of Row 1.

Repeat from ★ to last ch-3 sp, (ch 1, sc) three times in ch-3 sp, rotate project and working along the side of the project, (ch 1, sc) in each ch-2 sp at end of every other row to end, (ch 1, sc) twice around last sc, rotate project and working along the last row, (ch 1, sc) in each ch-1 sp to last ch-2 sp, (ch 1, sc) three times in ch-2 sp, rotate project and working along the side of the project, (ch 1, sc) in each ch-2 sp at end of every other row to end, ch 1, join with slip st to beginning ch 2, finish off.

With 2 strands of yarn held together, each 6" (15 cm) long, and using photo as a guide for placement, attach fringe evenly along short edges of Scarf ***(Figs. A & B)***. Trim ends evenly.

Fig. A

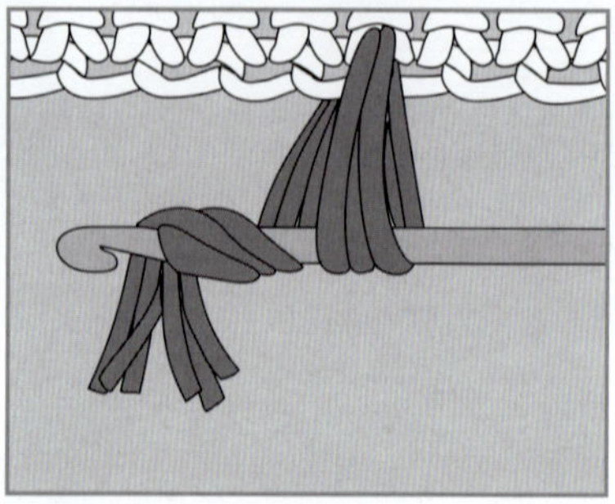

Fig. B

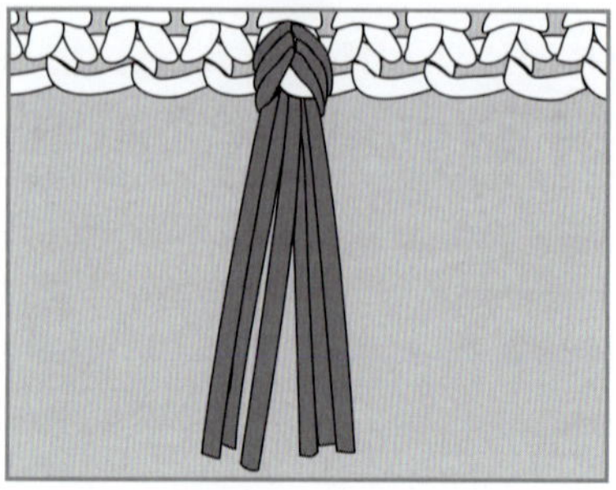

Weave in all loose ends.

Car Seat Cover

EASY

Finished Size: 25" x 37" (63.5 cm x 94 cm)

Shown on page 15.

SHOPPING LIST

Yarn (Medium Weight) 4

[4 ounces 204 yards
(113 grams, 187 meters) per skein]:

- ☐ Variegated - 5 skeins

[5 ounces, 256 yards
(141 grams, 234 meters) per skein]:

- ☐ White - 1 skein
- ☐ Purple - 1 skein
- ☐ Aqua - 1 skein

Crochet Hook

- ☐ Size J (6 mm)
  or size needed for gauge

Extra hooks in neighboring sizes
(see Planned Yarn Pooling, page 2)

Additional Supplies

- ☐ Yarn needle
- ☐ 1" (25 mm) buttons - 2
- ☐ Sewing needle and thread

GAUGE INFORMATION

In Moss St, 13 sts (sc and chs) and 13 rows = 4" (10 cm)

Gauge Swatch: 4" (10 cm) square

Ch 14.

Row 1: Skip 3 ch **(counts as a st)**, sc in next ch, ★ ch 1, skip 1 foundation ch, sc in next ch; repeat from ★ to end.

Row 2: Ch 2 **(counts as a st, now and throughout)**, turn; sc in next ch-1 sp, ★ ch 1, sc in next ch-1 sp; repeat from ★ to end finishing with a sc in last ch-3 sp.

Rows 3-13: Ch 2, turn; sc in next ch-1 sp, ★ ch 1, sc in next ch-1 sp; repeat from ★ to end finishing with a sc in last ch-2 sp.

Finish off.

STITCH GUIDE

MOSS STITCH *(abbreviated Moss St)*

Ch an even number of sts.

Row 1: Skip 3 ch **(counts as a st)**, sc in next ch, ★ ch 1, skip 1 foundation ch, sc in next ch; repeat from ★ to end, turn.

Row 2: Ch 2 **(counts as a st, now and throughout)**, turn; sc in next ch-1 sp, ★ ch 1, sc in next ch-1 sp; repeat from ★ to end finishing with a sc in last ch-3 sp.

Row 3: Ch 2, turn; sc in next ch-1 sp, ★ ch 1, sc in next ch-1 sp; repeat from ★ to end finishing with a sc in last ch-2 sp.

Repeat Row 3 for Moss St.

SURFACE SLIP STITCH *(abbreviated surface slip st)*

With yarn held on **wrong** side and hook on **right** side, insert hook in indicated st or sp, YO, pull loop to right side and through loop on hook.

COVER

With Variegated, ch through 2 full color sequences, with the last loop on hook being the first loop of a new color just after a color change in the yarn.

Row 1 (Right side)**:** Skip 3 ch **(counts as a st)**, sc in 4th ch from hook, ★ ch 1, sc around the foundation ch (instead of going into a ch st); repeat from ★ until 1 full color sequence has been completed. Count the number of sc made in each individual color in the colorway and note it down. Work 1½ more color sequences, maintaining the same number of sc made in each individual color. Leave remaining ch sts unworked. Undo one st repeat (sc, ch 1).

Note: Loop a short piece of yarn around any stitch to mark Row 1 as **right** side.

Row 2: Ch 2 **(counts as a st, now and throughout)**, turn; sc in next ch-1 sp, ★ ch 1, sc in next ch-1 sp; repeat from ★ to end, finishing with a sc in last ch-3 sp.

Note: As you work this row and all remaining rows, you MUST get the correct number of sc in each color in order to maintain the planned color pooling. Change hook sizes, or actual st used, to get the correct color in place. If you use the same number of sts per color that you counted on Row 1, it will work out.

Row 3: Ch 2, turn; sc in next ch-1 sp, ★ ch 1, sc in next ch-1 sp; repeat from ★ to end, finishing with a sc in last ch-2 sp.

Note: The color of the sts on this row will shift to the left or right by 1 st from the previous right side row depending on the colorway and if you are right or left handed. It doesn't matter which direction the stitch shifts as long as it is off-set by 1.

Row 4: Ch 2, turn; sc in next ch-1 sp, ★ ch 1, sc in next ch-1 sp; repeat from ★ to end, finishing with a sc in last ch-2 sp.

Note: The color of the sts on this row will shift to the left or right by 1 st from the previous wrong side row depending on the colorway and if you are right or left handed. It doesn't matter which direction the stitch shifts as long as it is off-set by 1.

Repeat Rows 3 and 4 until 4 full color repeats have been completed lengthwise, ending on a Row 3 (right side row).

FINISHING

Squish or stretch the sts on foundation chain to match the width of the rest of the Blanket. You can slide the sts around along the foundation chain, as with an adjustable ring. Unravel unused foundation ch sts and weave in yarn tail to secure foundation.

EDGING

Rnd 1: With **right** side facing and working across foundation edge, join White with slip st in foundation ch st under last sc of Row 1; ch 1, 2 sc in same ch as joining slip st, ★ 2 sc in next sp between sc of Row 1; repeat from ★ to ch-3 corner sp, 3 sc in corner sp, rotate Cover to work along long side edge, sc in each ch sp and sc at edge of every row to corner sc, 3 sc in corner sc, rotate Cover to work along top edge, 2 sc in each ch-1 sp to corner ch-2 sp, 3 sc in corner sp, rotate Cover to work along long side edge, sc in each ch sp and sc at edge of every other row to corner st, sc in corner st, join with slip st in beginning sc.

Rnd 2: Ch 1, 2 sc in same sp as joining slip st, ★ sc in each st to next corner, 3 sc in corner; repeat from ★ twice **more**, sc in same sp as first 2 sc, join with slip st in first sc.

Finish off.

Rnd 3: With **right** side facing, join Purple with slip st in corner sc, 2 sc in same sp as joining slip st, ★ sc in each st to next corner, 3 sc in corner; repeat from ★ twice **more**, sc in same sp as first 2 sc, join with slip st in first sc.

Next 4 Rnds: Ch 1, 2 sc in same st as joining slip st, sc in each sc to next corner st, ★ 3 sc in corner st, sc in each sc to next corner st; repeat from ★ twice more, sc in same st as first 2 sc, join with slip st in first sc.

Finish off.

TWISTED CHAIN BORDER

With **right** side facing, join White with sc in any sc ***(see Joining With Sc, page 31)***; ch 6, elongate loop on hook and remove hook, skip next sc, join Aqua with a sc in next sc, ch 6, elongate loop on hook and remove hook, ★ place White loop back on hook and bring it over Aqua ch-6, skip next sc, sc in next sc, ch 6, elongate loop on hook and remove hook, place Aqua loop back on hook and bring it over White ch-6, skip next sc, sc in next sc, ch 6, elongate loop on hook and remove hook; repeat from ★ around, join with slip st in the first sc of each color.

Finish off.

HANDLE STRAP

Place Cover on car seat to determine where the handle strap or straps should be, and whether they should be vertical or horizontal, and mark placement.

Work 4 sts in surface slip st for base of Strap.

Row 1: Ch 1, turn; sc in each slip st to end.

Row 2: Ch 2 **(does not count as a hdc)**, turn; working in Back Loop and horizontal loop, hdc in each st to end.

Rows 3-14: Repeat Row 2.

Row 15: Ch 1, turn; sc in each st to end.

Row 16 (buttonhole row)**:** Ch 1, turn; sc in first st, ch 2, skip next 2 sts, sc in last st.

Row 17: Ch 1, turn; sc in first sc, 2 sc in next ch-2 sp, sc in last sc.

Finish off.

FINISHING

Sew a button to base of each strap.

Weave in all loose ends.

Baby Cocoon

EASY

Finished Size: 24" circumference x 30" long (61 cm x 94 cm)

SHOPPING LIST

Yarn (Medium Weight) 4 MEDIUM

[5 ounces, 236 yards
(141 grams, 215 meters) per skein]:

☐ Variegated - 2 skein

[7 ounces, 364 yards
(198 grams, 333 meters) per skein]:

☐ Pink - 1 skein

Crochet Hook

☐ Size J (6 mm)
or size needed for gauge

Extra hooks in neighboring sizes
(see Planned Yarn Pooling, page 2)

Additional Supplies

☐ Split lock stitch markers

☐ Yarn needle

GAUGE INFORMATION

In Moss St, 13 sts (sc and chs) and 13 rows = 4" (10 cm)

Gauge Swatch: 4" (10 cm) square

Ch 14.

Row 1: Skip 3 ch **(counts as a st)**, sc in next ch, ★ ch 1, skip 1 foundation ch, sc in next ch; repeat from ★ to end.

Row 2: Ch 2 **(counts as a st, now and throughout)**, turn; sc in next ch-1 sp, ★ ch 1, sc in next ch-1 sp; repeat from ★ to end finishing with a sc in last ch-3 sp.

Rows 3-13: Ch 2, turn; sc in next ch-1 sp, ★ ch 1, sc in next ch-1 sp; repeat from ★ to end finishing with a sc in last ch-2 sp.

Finish off.

STITCH GUIDE

MOSS STITCH *(abbreviated Moss St)*

Ch an even number of sts.

Row 1: Skip 3 ch **(counts as a st)**, sc in next ch, ★ ch 1, skip 1 foundation ch, sc in next ch; repeat from ★ to end, turn.

Row 2: Ch 2 **(counts as a st, now and throughout)**, turn; sc in next ch-1 sp, ★ ch 1, sc in next ch-1 sp; repeat from ★ to end finishing with a sc in last ch-3 sp.

Row 3: Ch 2, turn; sc in next ch-1 sp, ★ ch 1, sc in next ch-1 sp; repeat from ★ to end finishing with a sc in last ch-2 sp.

Repeat Row 3 for Moss St.

CROCHET MAGIC RING

Wrap yarn around your left middle finger twice, leaving a 6" (15 cm) tail. Insert hook under both strands, and pull up a loop. Ch 1, and begin working directly into center of ring. This ring can be tightened later by pulling on the yarn tail ***(Figs. 1a-d, page 31)***.

SINGLE CROCHET 2 TOGETHER *(abbreviated sc2tog)*

Pull up a loop in each of next 2 sts, YO and draw through all 3 loops on hook **(counts as one sc)**.

COCOON BODY

With Variegated, ch through 3 full color sequences, with the last loop on hook being the first loop of a new color just after a color change in the yarn.

Row 1 (Right side)**:** Skip 3 ch **(counts as a st)**, sc in the 4th ch from hook, ★ ch 1, sc around the foundation ch (instead of going into a ch st); repeat from ★ until 1 full color sequence has been completed. Count the number of sc made in each individual color in the colorway and note it down. Work 2 more color sequences, maintaining the same number of sc made in each individual color. Leave remaining ch sts unworked. Undo one st repeat (sc, ch 1).

Note: Loop a short piece of yarn around any stitch to mark Row 1 as **right** side.

Row 2: Ch 2 **(counts as a st, now and throughout)**, turn; sc in next ch-1 sp, ★ ch 1, sc in next ch-1 sp; repeat from ★ to end finishing with a sc in last ch-3 sp.

Note: As you work this row and all remaining rows, you MUST get the correct number of sc in each color in order to maintain the planned color pooling. Change hook sizes, or actual st used, to get the correct color in place. If you use the same number of sts per color that you counted on Row 1, it will work out.

Row 3: Ch 2, turn; sc in next ch-1 sp, ★ ch 1, sc in the next ch-1 sp; repeat from ★ to end, finishing with a sc in last ch-2 sp.

Note: The color of the sts on this row will shift to the left or right by 1 st from the previous right side row depending on the colorway and if you are right or left handed. It doesn't matter which direction the stitch shifts as long as it is off-set by 1.

Row 4: Ch 2, turn; sc in next ch-1 sp, ★ ch 1, sc in the next ch-1 sp; repeat from ★ to end, finishing with a sc in last ch-2 sp.

Note: The color of the sts on this row will shift to the left or right by 1 st from the previous wrong side row depending on the colorway and if you are right or left handed. It doesn't matter which direction the stitch shifts as long as it is off-set by 1. Repeat Rows 3 and 4 until piece measures 28" (71 cm), ending on a Row 4 (wrong side row).

1st FINISHING

Squish or stretch the sts on foundation chain to match the width of the rest of the Body. You can slide the sts around along the foundation chain, as with an adjustable ring. Unravel unused foundation ch sts and weave in yarn tail to secure foundation.

Sew side edges together with **wrong** side facing.

BASE

Rnd 1: With **right** side facing, join Pink with slip st in any sp along foundation edge, ch 1, sc in same sp, 59 more sc evenly around edge, join with slip st in first sc.
Place a marker in every 10th st around – 6 markers placed.

Rnd 2: Ch 1, ★ sc in each sc to 1 st before marked st, sc2tog over next 2 sts, move marker to sc2tog just made; repeat from ★ 5 **more** times, join with slip st in first sc – 54 sc.

Rnds 3-9: Repeat Rnd 2 – 12 sts at end of Rnd 9.

Rnd 10: Ch 1, (sc2tog over next 2 sts) 6 times.

Finish off, leaving a long tail.

EDGING

Rnd 1: With **right** side facing, join Pink with slip st in any sp along top edge, ch 2 **(does not count as a st, now and throughout)**, hdc in each st and sp around, join with slip st in beginning ch-2.

Rnds 2-4: Ch 2 , turn, hdc in each hdc around, join with slip st in beginning ch-2.

Work 1 rnd in reverse sc ***(Figs. 2a-d, page 31)***, join with slip st to first st, finish off.

FLOWER EMBELLISHMENT

Create a Magic Ring.

Rnd 1: Ch 1, 8 sc in ring, join with slip st in first sc.

Rnd 2: Ch 5 **(counts as 1 dc and 2 ch)**, ★ skip next sc, dc in next sc, ch 2; repeat from ★ 6 **more** times, join with slip st in 3rd of beginning ch-5.

Rnd 3: Slip st in next sp, ch 1, (sc, hdc, dc, hdc, sc, ch 1) in same sp and in each sp around, join with slip st in first sc.

Finish off.

2nd FINISHING

Thread yarn tail at center of Base through darning needle, and weave through sts of final round. Pull tight, closing hole at center.
Sew flower embellishment onto cocoon as shown in photo, or as desired.

Weave in all loose ends.

Hooded Scarf

EASY

Finished Sizes:
Scarf - 80" long x 7½" wide (203 cm x 19) cm
Hood - 18" x 17½" (46 cm x 45 cm)

SHOPPING LIST

Yarn (Medium Weight) 4

[3 ounces, 146 yards
(85 grams, 134 meters) per skein]:
☐ Variegated - 9 skein
[7 ounces 364 yards
(198 grams, 333 meters) per skein]:
☐ Red - 1 skein

Crochet Hook

☐ Size J (6 mm)
or size needed for gauge
Extra hooks in neighboring sizes
(see Planned Yarn Pooling, page 2)

Additional Supplies

☐ Split lock stitch markers
☐ Yarn needle

GAUGE INFORMATION

In Moss St, 13 sts (sc and chs) and 13 rows = 4" (10 cm)
Gauge Swatch: 4" (10 cm) square
Ch 14.
Row 1: Skip 3 ch **(counts as a st)**, sc in next ch, ★ ch 1, skip 1 foundation ch, sc in next ch; repeat from ★ to end.
Row 2: Ch 2 **(counts as a st, now and throughout)**, turn; sc in next ch-1 sp, ★ ch 1, sc in next ch-1 sp; repeat from ★ to end finishing with a sc in last ch-3 sp.
Rows 3-13: Ch 2, turn; sc in next ch-1 sp, ★ ch 1, sc in next ch-1 sp; repeat from ★ to end finishing with a sc in last ch-2 sp.
Finish off.

STITCH GUIDE

MOSS STITCH *(abbreviated Moss St)*
Ch an even number of sts.
Row 1: Skip 3 ch **(counts as a st)**, sc in next ch, ★ ch 1, skip 1 foundation ch, sc in next ch; repeat from ★ to end, turn.
Row 2: Ch 2 **(counts as a st, now and throughout)**, turn; sc in next ch-1 sp, ★ ch 1, sc in next ch-1 sp; repeat from ★ to end finishing with a sc in last ch-3 sp.
Row 3: Ch 2, turn; sc in next ch-1 sp, ★ ch 1, sc in next ch-1 sp; repeat from ★ to end finishing with a sc in last ch-2 sp.
Repeat Row 3 for Moss St.
SINGLE CROCHET 2 TOGETHER *(abbreviated sc2tog)*
Pull up a loop in each of next 2 sts, YO and draw through all 3 loops on hook **(counts as one sc)**.

SCARF

With A, ch through 9 full color sequences, with the last loop on hook being the first loop of a new color just after a color change in the yarn.

Row 1 (Right side)**:** Skip 3 ch **(counts as a st)**, sc in the 4th ch from hook, ★ ch 1, sc around the foundation ch (instead of going into a ch st); repeat from ★ until 1 full color sequence has been completed. Count the number of sc made in each individual color in the colorway and note it down. Work 8 more full color sequences, maintaining the same number of sc made in each individual color. Leave remaining ch sts unworked. Undo one st repeat (sc, ch 1).

Note: Loop a short piece of yarn around any stitch to mark Row 1 as **right** side.

Row 2: Ch 2 **(counts as a st, now and throughout)**, turn; sc in next ch-1 sp, ★ ch 1, sc in next ch-1 sp; repeat from ★ to end finishing with a sc in last ch-3 sp.

Note: As you work this row and all remaining rows, you MUST get the correct number of sc in each color in order to maintain the planned color pooling. Change hook sizes, or actual st used, to get the correct color in place. If you use the same number of sts per color that you counted on Row 1, it will work out.

Row 3: Ch 2, turn; sc in next ch-1 sp, ★ ch 1, sc in the next ch-1 sp; repeat from ★ to end, finishing with a sc in last ch-2 sp.

Note: The color of the sts on this row will shift to the left or right by 1 st from the previous right side row depending on the colorway and if you are right or left handed. It doesn't matter which direction the stitch shifts as long as it is off-set by 1.

Row 4: Ch 2, turn; sc in next ch-1 sp, ★ ch 1, sc in the next ch-1 sp; repeat from ★ to end, finishing with a sc in last ch-2 sp.

Note: The color of the sts on this row will shift to the left or right by 1 st from the previous wrong side row depending on the colorway and if you are right or left handed. It doesn't matter which direction the stitch shifts as long as it is off-set by 1.

Repeat Rows 3 and 4 until piece measures 6½" (16.5 cm), ending on a Row 3 (right side row).

Finish off.

HOOD

Place a marker at center sp of top most row, then place 2 additional markers at spaces 1 color sequence away on either side. Remove center marker.

With **right** side facing, join yarn with slip st in first marked sp. Try to join the yarn at the correct spot in the new yarn's color sequence in order to keep the pooling continuous. This may take a couple of tries.

Row 1: Ch 2, sc in next ch-1 sp, ★ ch 1, sc in the next ch-1 sp; repeat from ★, keeping color pooling intact, until 2 full color sequences have been completed. Leave remaining sts unworked. Undo one st repeat (sc, ch 1), turn.

Remove markers, and continue as established across Hood portion only until Hood measures 17¼" (44 cm) from foundation row.

Finish off.

FINISHING

Squish or stretch the sts on foundation chain to match the width of the rest of the piece. You can slide the sts around along the foundation chain, as with an adjustable ring. Unravel unused foundation ch sts and weave in yarn tail to secure foundation.

SEAM HOOD

Join Variegated with slip st in final sc of Hood, then sc in ch sp at other corner.

★ Sc in next ch sp nearest first corner, sc in next ch sp nearest second corner; repeat from ★ to center of Hood.

Finish off.

EDGING

With **wrong** side facing, join Red with slip st in first corner along bottom of Scarf.

Rnd 1: Ch 1, (sc, ch 1) twice in same corner st, ★ (sc in next sp, ch 1) to next corner, (sc, ch 1) twice in corner st; repeat from ★ 2 **more** times, (sc in next sp, ch 1) to Hood, sc2tog, (sc in next sp, ch 1) to Scarf, sc2tog, (sc in next sp, ch 1) to next corner, (sc, ch 1) twice in corner st, (sc in next sp, ch 1) to end, join with slip st in beginning ch-2, finish off.

Weave in all loose ends.

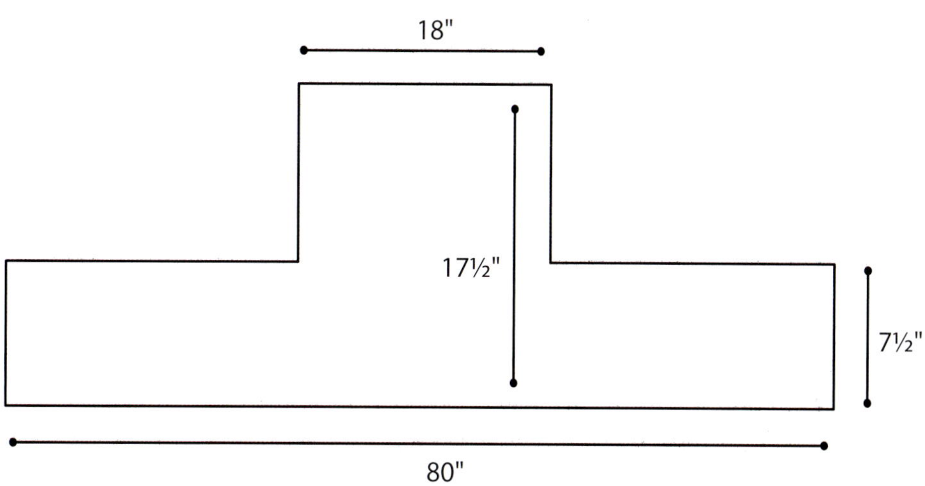

CHILD'S SWEATER

EASY

SHOPPING LIST

Yarn (Medium Weight) MEDIUM 4

[4 ounces 204 yards
(113 grams, 187 meters) per skein]:

- ☐ Variegated - 2{3-4} skeins

[5 ounces, 256 yards
(141 grams, 234 meters) per skein]:

- ☐ Orange - 1{2-2} skein(s)

Crochet Hook

- ☐ Size J (6 mm)
  or size needed for gauge

Extra hooks in neighboring sizes
(see Planned Yarn Pooling, page 2)

Additional Supplies

- ☐ Split lock stitch markers
- ☐ Yarn needle

SIZE INFORMATION

Chest Measurement:
24{28-32}"/61{71-81.5} cm
Length: 14¼{17-19½}"/
36{43-49.5} cm

Size Note: We have printed the instructions for the sizes in dirrerent colors to make it easier for you to find:

- Size 2 in Aqua
- Size 4 in Pink
- Size 6 in Green

Instructions in Black apply to all sizes.

GAUGE INFORMATION

In Moss St, 13 sts (sc and chs) and 13 rows = 4" (10 cm)
Gauge Swatch: 4" (10 cm) square
Ch 14.
Row 1: Skip 3 ch **(counts as a st)**, sc in next ch, ★ ch 1, skip 1 foundation ch, sc in next ch; repeat from ★ to end.
Row 2: Ch 2 **(counts as a st, now and throughout)**, turn; sc in next ch-1 sp, ★ ch 1, sc in next ch-1 sp; repeat from ★ to end finishing with a sc in last ch-3 sp.
Rows 3-13: Ch 2, turn; sc in next ch-1 sp, ★ ch 1, sc in next ch-1 sp; repeat from ★ to end finishing with a sc in last ch-2 sp.
Finish off.

STITCH GUIDE

MOSS STITCH *(abbreviated Moss St)*
Ch an even number of sts.
Row 1: Skip 3 ch **(counts as a st)**, sc in next ch, ★ ch 1, skip 1 foundation ch, sc in next ch; repeat from ★ to end, turn.
Row 2: Ch 2 **(counts as a st, now and throughout)**, turn; sc in next ch-1 sp, ★ ch 1, sc in next ch-1 sp; repeat from ★ to end finishing with a sc in last ch-3 sp.
Row 3: Ch 2, turn; sc in next ch-1 sp, ★ ch 1, sc in next ch-1 sp; repeat from ★ to end finishing with a sc in last ch-2 sp.
Repeat Row 3 for Moss St.
SINGLE CROCHET 2 TOGETHER *(abbreviated sc2tog)*
Pull up a loop in each of next 2 sts, YO and draw through all 3 loops on hook **(counts as one sc)**.

BODY

With Variegated, ch through 3{4-4} full color sequences, with the last loop on hook being the first loop of a new color just after a color change in the yarn.

Rnd 1 (Right side): Skip 3 ch **(counts as a st)**, sc in the 4th ch from hook, ★ ch 1, sc around the foundation ch (instead of going into a ch st); repeat from ★ until 1 full color sequence has been completed. Count the number of sc made in each individual color in the colorway and note it down. Work 2{2½-3} more color sequences, maintaining the same number of sc made in each individual color. Leave remaining ch sts unworked. Undo one st repeat (sc, ch 1), join with slip st in first sp.

Note: Loop a short piece of yarn around any stitch to mark Rnd 1 as **right** side.

Rnd 2: Ch 2 **(counts as a st, now and throughout)**, turn; sc in next ch-1 sp, ★ ch 1, sc in next ch-1 sp; repeat from ★ to end finishing with a sc in last ch-3 sp, join with slip st in first sp.

Note: As you work this rnd and all remaining rnds, you MUST get the correct number of sc in each color in order to maintain the planned color pooling. Change hook sizes, or actual st used, to get the correct color in place. If you use the same number of sts per color that you counted on Rnd 1, it will work out.

Rnd 3: Ch 2, turn; sc in next ch-1 sp, ★ ch 1, sc in the next ch-1 sp; repeat from ★ to end, finishing with a sc in last ch-2 sp, join with slip st in first sp.

Note: The color of the sts on this rnd will shift to the left or right by 1 st from the previous right side rnd depending on the colorway and if you are right or left handed. It doesn't matter which direction the stitch shifts as long as it is off-set by 1.

Rnd 4: Ch 2, turn; sc in next ch-1 sp, ★ ch 1, sc in the next ch-1 sp; repeat from ★ to end, finishing with a sc in last ch-2 sp, join with slip st in first sp.

Note: The color of the sts on this rnd will shift to the left or right by 1 st from the previous wrong side rnd depending on the colorway and if you are right or left handed. It doesn't matter which direction the stitch shifts as long as it is off-set by 1.

Repeat Rnds 3 and 4 until piece measures 8{9½-11}"/20.5{24-28} cm.

Finish off.

1st FINISHING

Squish or stretch the sts on foundation chain to match the width of the rest of the piece. You can slide the sts around along the foundation chain, as with an adjustable ring. Unravel unused foundation ch sts and weave in yarn tail to secure foundation.

SLEEVE (Make 2)

With Orange, ch 20{24-28}, and work 4 rows in Moss St – 18{22-26} sts across.

Next Row (Increase row)**:** Ch 2, (sc, ch 1) in each sp to center sp, (sc, ch 1) twice in center sp, (sc, ch 1) in each sp to last sp, sc in last sp, turn – 20{24-28} sts.

Working in Moss St, repeat this increase every 6{8-10} rows, 3{4-4} **more** times – 26{32-36} sts.

Work 9{5-7} more rows evenly, then finish off.

RAGLAN YOKE

Place a marker in first sp of last row of Body, and another marker halfway around Body.

Rnd 1: With **right** side facing, join Orange with slip st in ch-1 sp halfway between markers, ch 2, (sc, ch 1) in each sp to first marker and mark last ch made, (sc, ch 1) in each sp across one Sleeve and mark last ch st made, (sc, ch 1) in each sp on Body to second marker and mark last ch made, (sc, ch 1) in each sp across other sleeve and mark last ch st made, (sc, ch 1) in each remaining sp on Body placing final sc in same sp as joining slip st, join with slip st in first ch-2 sp.

Rnd 2: Ch 2, turn; (sc, ch 1) in each sp around placing final sc in same sp as joining slip st, join with slip st in first ch-2 sp. Move each marker to st immediately above it.

Rnds 3 and 4 (Decrease rnds)**:** Ch 2, turn; ★ (sc, ch 1) in each sp to last sp before marked st, sc2tog over next 2 sps skipping the sc between them, ch 1; repeat from ★ 3 **more** times, (sc, ch 1) in each remaining sp to end placing final sc in same sp as joining slip st, join with slip st in first ch-2 sp. Move each marker to st immediately above it.

Rnds 5 and 6: Ch 2, turn; (sc, ch 1) in each sp around placing final sc in same sp as joining slip st, join with slip st in first ch-2 sp.

Repeat Rnds 3-6, 3{4-5} **more** times, then repeat Rnd 3 only once **more**.

Finish off.

2nd FINISHING

Join Sleeve seams as follows:
With **wrong** side together, join Orange with slip st at cuff corner opposite the final row's ch sp, then sc in this ch sp.
★ Sc in next row-edge sp on first edge, sc in next row-edge sp on second edge; repeat from ★ to underarm, finish off.

Repeat for second Sleeve.

CUFFS AND NECK EDGE

With **right** side facing, join Variegated with slip st in any sp along Cuff edge.
Working from **left** to **right**, work reverse sc around ***(Figs. 2a-d, page 31)***; join with slip st to first st, then finish off.

Work other Cuff and Neck Edge the same way.

BOTTOM EDGE

Rnd 1: With **right** side facing, join Orange with slip st in any sp along bottom edge; ch 2, (sc, ch 1) in each sp around, join with slip st in first sp.
Working from **left** to **right**, work reverse sc around; join with slip st to first st, then finish off.

Weave in all loose ends.

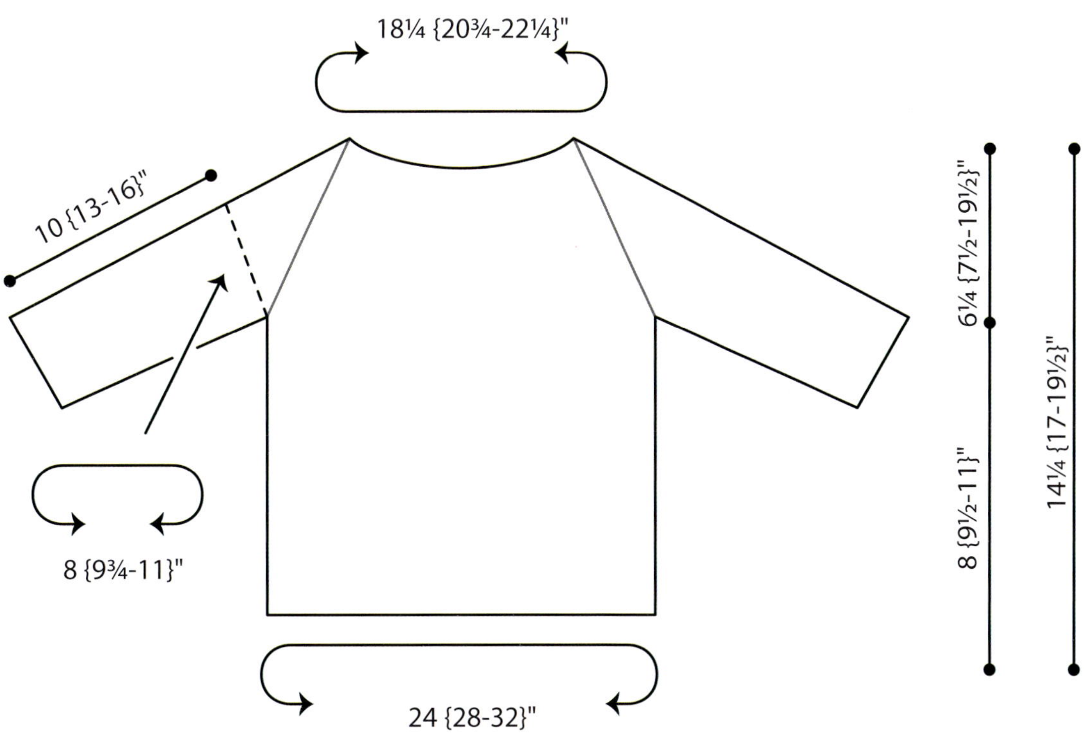

Poncho With Raglan Yoke

EASY

SHOPPING LIST

Yarn (Medium Weight) 4

[7 ounces 364 yards
(198 grams, 333 meters) per skein]:

- ☐ Brown - 3{4-5-6} skeins

[5 ounces, 236 yards
(141 grams, 215 meters) per skein]:

- ☐ Variegated - 3{3-4-4} skeins

Crochet Hook

- ☐ Size J (6 mm)
  or size needed for gauge

Extra hooks in neighboring sizes
(see Planned Yarn Pooling, page 2)

Additional Supplies

- ☐ Split lock stitch markers
- ☐ Yarn needle

SIZE INFORMATION

Trim circumference:
66¼{71½-78¾-83¾}"/
168.5{181.5-200-212.5} cm
Neck: 29½{32-34½-37}"/
75{81.5-87.5-94} cm
Length: 26{28½-31-33½}"/
66{72.5-78.5-85} cm

Size Note: We have printed the instructions for the sizes in different colors to make it easier for you to find:

- Size Small in Aqua
- Size Medium in Pink
- Size Large/1X in Green
- Size 2X in Red

GAUGE INFORMATION

In Moss St, 13 sts (sc and chs) and 13 rows = 4" (10 cm)
Gauge Swatch: 4" (10 cm) square
Ch 14.
Row 1: Skip 3 ch **(counts as a st)**, sc in next ch, ★ ch 1, skip 1 foundation ch, sc in next ch; repeat from ★ to end.
Row 2: Ch 2 **(counts as a st, now and throughout)**, turn; sc in next ch-1 sp, ★ ch 1, sc in next ch-1 sp; repeat from ★ to end finishing with a sc in last ch-3 sp.
Rows 3-13: Ch 2, turn; sc in next ch-1 sp, ★ ch 1, sc in next ch-1 sp; repeat from ★ to end finishing with a sc in last ch-2 sp.
Finish off.

STITCH GUIDE

MOSS STITCH *(abbreviated Moss St)*
Ch an even number of sts.
Row 1: Skip 3 ch **(counts as a st)**, sc in next ch, ★ ch 1, skip 1 foundation ch, sc in next ch; repeat from ★ to end, turn.
Row 2: Ch 2 **(counts as a st, now and throughout)**, turn; sc in next ch-1 sp, ★ ch 1, sc in next ch-1 sp; repeat from ★ to end finishing with a sc in last ch-3 sp.
Row 3: Ch 2, turn; sc in next ch-1 sp, ★ ch 1, sc in next ch-1 sp; repeat from ★ to end finishing with a sc in last ch-2 sp.
Repeat Row 3 for Moss St.

SINGLE CROCHET 2 TOGETHER *(abbreviated sc2tog)*
Pull up a loop in each of next 2 sc, YO and draw through all 3 loops on hook **(counts as one sc)**.

PONCHO

COLOR-POOLED TRIM

With Variegated, ch through at least 1 full color sequence, with the last loop on hook being the first loop of a new color just after a color change in the yarn.

Row 1 (Right side)**:** Skip 3 ch **(counts as a st)**, sc in the 4th ch from hook, ★ ch 1, sc around the foundation ch (instead of going into a ch st); repeat from ★ until 1 full color sequence has been completed. Count the number of sc made in each individual color in the colorway and note it down. Leave remaining ch sts unworked. Undo one st repeat (sc, ch 1), turn.

Note: Loop a short piece of yarn around any stitch to mark Row 1 as **right** side.

Row 2: Ch 2 **(counts as a st, now and throughout)**, turn; sc in next ch-1 sp, ★ ch 1, sc in next ch-1 sp; repeat from ★ to end finishing with a sc in last ch-3 sp.

Note: As you work this row and all remaining rows, you MUST get the correct number of sc in each color in order to maintain the planned color pooling. Change hook sizes, or actual st used, to get the correct color in place. If you use the same number of sts per color that you counted on Row 1, it will work out.

Row 3: Ch 2, turn; sc in next ch-1 sp, ★ ch 1, sc in the next ch-1 sp; repeat from ★ to end, finishing with a sc in last ch-2 sp.

Note: The color of the sts on this row will shift to the left or right by 1 st from the previous right side row depending on the colorway and if you are right or left handed. It doesn't matter which direction the stitch shifts as long as it is off-set by 1.

Row 4: Ch 2, turn; sc in next ch-1 sp, ★ ch 1, sc in the next ch-1 sp; repeat from ★ to end, finishing with a sc in last ch-2 sp.

Note: The color of the sts on this row will shift to the left or right by 1 st from the previous wrong side row depending on the colorway and if you are right or left handed. It doesn't matter which direction the stitch shifts as long as it is off-set by 1.

Repeat Rows 3 and 4 until Trim measures 66¼{71½-78¾-83¾}"/ 168.5{181.5-200-212.5} cm ending on a Row 4 (wrong side row).

FInish off.

TRIM FINISHIING

Squish or stretch the sts on foundation chain to match the width of the rest of the piece. You can slide the sts around along the foundation chain, as with an adjustable ring. Unravel unused foundation ch sts and weave in yarn tail to secure foundation.

With **wrong** side facing and working across the foundation chain edge, join Variegated with slip st in ch-3 edge sp, ch 1, sc in same sp, ★ ch 1, sc in next sp between sc of Row 1; repeat from ★ to end of foundation edge, ch 1, slip st in foundation ch st under last sc of Row 1.

Finish off.

Sew together short edges of Trim.

Note: Measure average gauge of Trim. At this point it is more important for the Body gauge to match the Trim gauge than the gauge listed in this pattern.

BODY

With **right** side facing and working across one long side edge of Trim, join Brown with slip st any edge sp, and work Body in joined and turned rounds as follows:

Rnd 1: Ch 2, sc in next sp, ★ ch 1, sc in the next sp; repeat from ★ around, finishing with a sc in same sp as joining slip st, join with a slip st in beginning ch-2 sp.

Rnds 2-7: Ch 2, turn; sc in next sp, ★ ch 1, sc in the next sp; repeat from ★ around, finishing with a sc in same sp as joining slip st, join with a slip st in beginning ch-2 sp.

Place 4 markers in 4 evenly-spaced sc sts across last worked round.

Rnd 8 (Decrease rnd)**:** Ch 2, turn; sc in next sp, ★ (ch 1, sc in the next sp) to last sp before next marked st, sc2tog over next 2 sps skipping marked sc between them, move marker to sc2tog just made, ch 1; repeat from ★ 3 **more** times, (ch 1, sc in the next sp) to end of round, finishing with a sc in same sp as joining slip st, join with a slip st in beginning ch-2 sp.

Rnds 9 and 11: Repeat Rnd 2. Move each marker to mark sp directly above it.

Rnds 10 and 12: Repeat Rnd 2. Move each marker to mark to sc directly above it.

Rnd 13 (Decrease rnd)**:** Repeat Rnd 8.

(Work 4 rounds evenly, moving markers up with each round, then work a decrease round) 1{3-5-7} **more** time(s).

(Work 2 rounds evenly, moving markers up with each round, then work a decrease rnd) until 96{104-112-120} sts [48{52-56-60} sc] or fewer remain.

Remove all markers.

Next 2 Rnds: Ch 1, sc in each st around, join with slip st in first sc.

Next Rnd: Ch 2 **(does not count as a st)**, hdc in each sc around, join with slip st in first hdc.

Finish off.

Edging: With **right** side facing, join Variegated with slip st in any hdc, work 1 rnd in reverse sc ***(Figs. 2a-d, page 31)***, join with slip st in first sc. Finish off.

Weave in all loose ends.

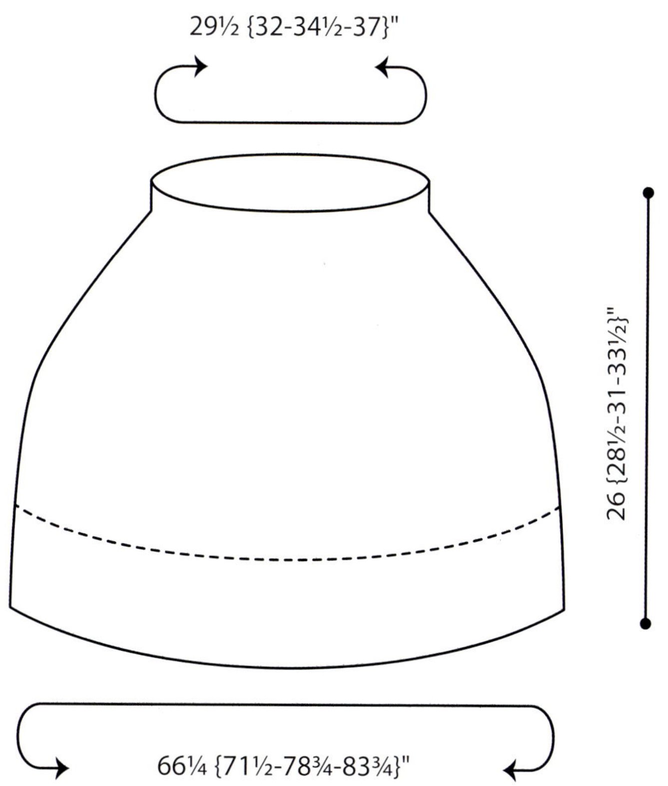

General Instructions

ABBREVIATIONS

ch(s)	chain(s)
cm	centimeters
dc	double crochet(s)
mm	millimeters
Rnd(s)	Round(s)
sc	single crochet(s)
sc2tog	single crochet 2 together
sp(s)	space(es)
st(s)	stitch(es)
YO	yarn over

SYMBOLS & TERMS

★ — work instructions following ★ as many **more** times as indicated in addition to the first time.

( ) or **[ ]** — work enclosed instructions **as many** times as specified by the number immediately following **or** contains explanatory remarks.

colon (:) — the number(s) given after a colon at the end of a row or round denote(s) the number of stitches you should have on that row or round.

GAUGE

Exact gauge is **essential** for proper size. Before beginning your project, make the sample swatch given in the individual instructions in the yarn and hook specified. After completing the swatch, measure it, counting your stitches and rows carefully. If your swatch is larger or smaller than specified, **make another, changing hook size to get the correct gauge.** Keep trying until you find the size hook that will give you the specified gauge.

CROCHET TERMINOLOGY

UNITED STATES		INTERNATIONAL
slip stitch (slip st)	=	single crochet (sc)
single crochet (sc)	=	double crochet (dc)
half double crochet (hdc)	=	half treble crochet (htr)
double crochet (dc)	=	treble crochet (tr)
treble crochet (tr)	=	double treble crochet (dtr)
double treble crochet (dtr)	=	triple treble crochet (ttr)
triple treble crochet (tr tr)	=	quadruple treble crochet (qtr)
skip	=	miss

Yarn Weight Symbol & Names	LACE 0	SUPER FINE 1	FINE 2	LIGHT 3	MEDIUM 4	BULKY 5	SUPER BULKY 6	JUMBO 7
Type of Yarns in Category	Fingering, size 10 crochet thread	Sock, Fingering, Baby	Sport, Baby	DK, Light Worsted	Worsted, Afghan, Aran	Chunky, Craft, Rug	Super Bulky, Roving	Jumbo, Roving
Crochet Gauge* Ranges in Single Crochet to 4" (10 cm)	32-42 sts**	21-32 sts	16-20 sts	12-17 sts	11-14 sts	8-11 sts	6-9 sts	5 sts and fewer
Advised Hook Size Range	Steel*** 6 to 8, Regular hook B-1	B-1 to E-4	E-4 to 7	7 to I-9	I-9 to K-10½	K-10½ to M/N-13	M/N-13 to Q	Q and larger

*GUIDELINES ONLY: The chart above reflects the most commonly used gauges and hook sizes for specific yarn categories.

** Lace weight yarns are usually crocheted with larger hooks to create lacy openwork patterns. Accordingly, a gauge range is difficult to determine. Always follow the gauge stated in your pattern.

*** Steel crochet hooks are sized differently from regular hooks–the higher the number, the smaller the hook, which is the reverse of regular hook sizing.

BEGINNER	Projects for first-time crocheters using basic stitches. Minimal shaping.
EASY	Projects using yarn with basic stitches, repetitive stitch patterns, simple color changes, and simple shaping and finishing.
INTERMEDIATE	Projects using a variety of techniques, such as basic lace patterns or color patterns, mid-level shaping and finishing.
EXPERIENCED	Projects with intricate stitch patterns, techniques and dimension, such as non-repeating patterns, multi-color techniques, fine threads, small hooks, detailed shaping and refined finishing.

JOINING WITH SC

When instructed to join with sc, begin with a slip knot on hook. Insert hook in stitch or space indicated, YO and pull up a loop, YO and draw through both loops on hook.

CROCHET MAGIC RING

Wind yarn around two fingers to form a ring ***(Fig. 1a)***. Slide yarn off fingers and grasp the strands at the top of the ring ***(Fig. 1b)***. Insert hook from **front** to **back** into the ring, pull up a loop, YO and draw through loop on hook to lock ring ***(Fig. 1c)*** (st made does **not** count as part of beginning ch). Working around both strands, follow instructions to work sts in the ring, then pull yarn tail to close ***(Fig. 1d)***.

Fig. 1a

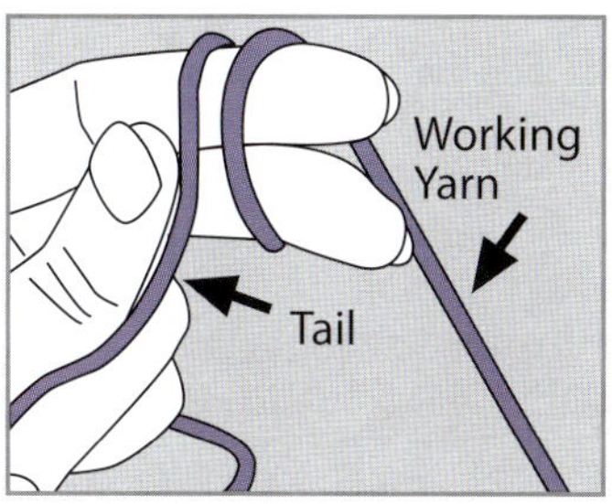

Fig. 1b

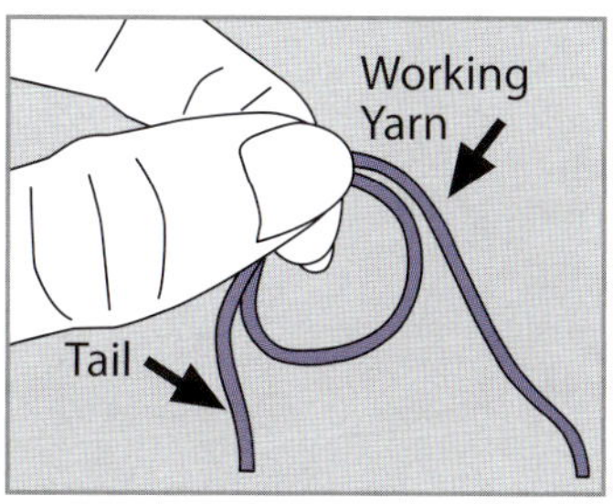

Fig. 1c

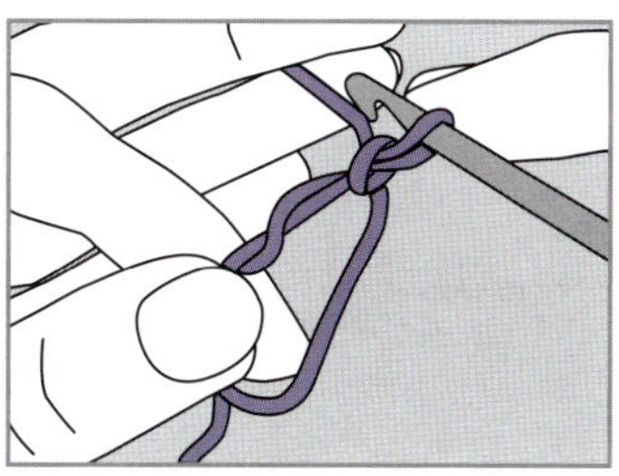

Fig. 1d

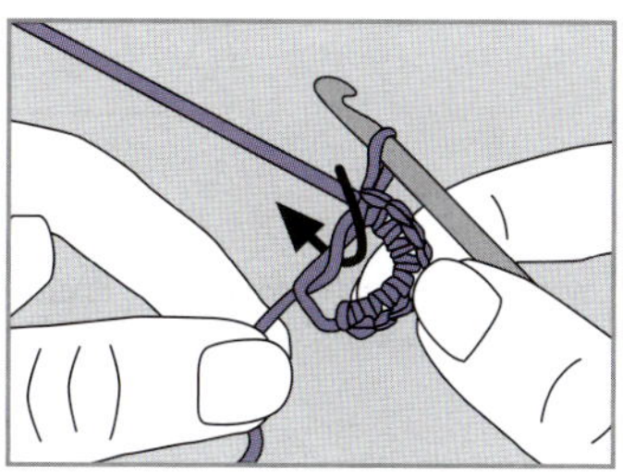

REVERSE SINGLE CROCHET

(abbreviated reverse sc)

Working from **left** to **right**, ★ insert hook in st to right of hook ***(Fig. 2a)***, YO and draw through, under and to left of loop on hook (2 loops on hook) ***(Fig. 2b)***, YO and draw through both loops on hook ***(Fig. 2c)*** **(reverse sc made, *Fig. 2d*)**; repeat from ★ around; join with slip st to first st, finish off.

Fig. 2a

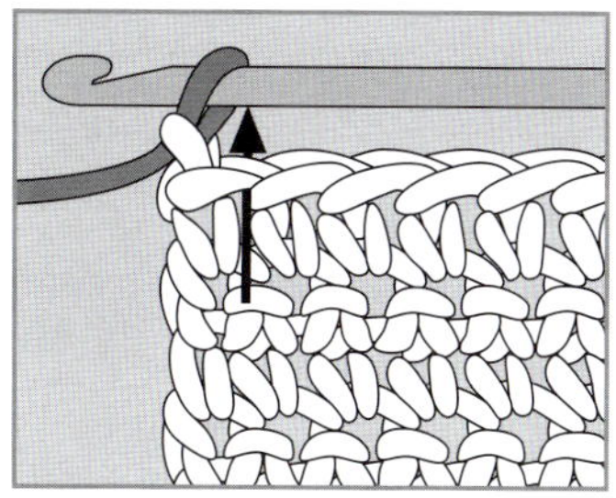

Fig. 2b

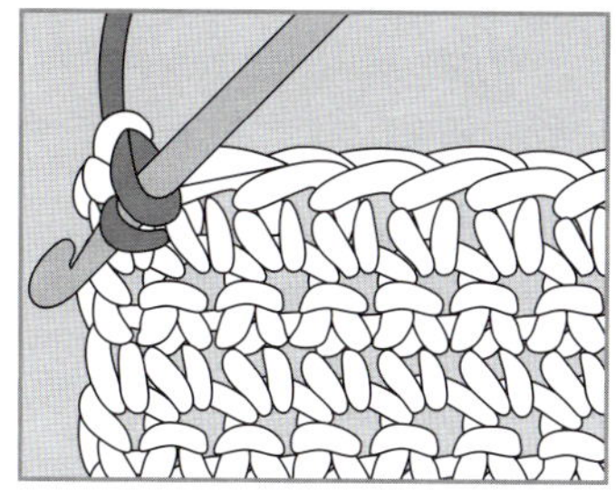

Fig. 2c

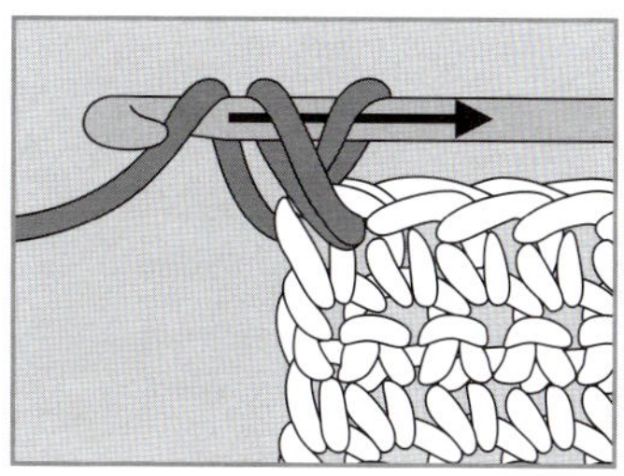

Fig. 2d

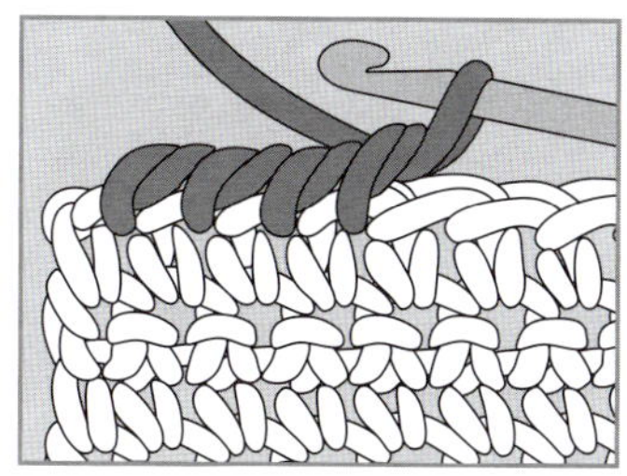

CROCHET HOOKS																	
U.S.	B-1	C-2	D-3	E-4	F-5	G-6	7	H-8	I-9	J-10	K-10½	L-11	M/N-13	N/P-15	P/Q	Q	S
Metric - mm	2.25	2.75	3.25	3.5	3.75	4	4.5	5	5.5	6	6.5	8	9	10	15	16	19

Yarn Information

The items in this book were made using Medium Weight yarn. Any brand of the specified yarn weight may be used. It is best to refer to the yardage/meters when determining how many balls or skeins to purchase. Remember, to arrive at the finished size, it is the GAUGE/TENSION that is important, not the brand of yarn.

For your convenience, listed below are the specific yarns used to create our photography models. Because yarn manufacturers make frequent changes in their product lines, you may sometimes find it necessary to use a substitute yarn or to search for the discontinued product at alternate suppliers (locally or online).

FULL SCARF
Red Heart® Super Saver®
#906 Heartfelt

WRISTLETS, COWL, & HAT SET
Red Heart® Super Saver®
Variegated - #3952 Icelandic Mix
Grey - #400 Grey Heather

ZIG-ZAG SCARF
Red Heart® Super Saver®
Variegated - #932 Zebra
Black - #312 Black

CAR SEAT COVER
Red Heart® Soft Baby Steps®
Variegated - #9939 Tickle
White - #9600 White
Purple - #9536 Light Grape
Aqua - #9505 Aqua

COCOON
Red Heart® Super Saver®
Variegated - #972 Pink Camo
Pink - #774 Light Raspberry

HOODED SCARF
Red Heart® Classic®
Variegated - #996 Sedona
Red Heart® Super Saver®
Red - #332 Ranch Red

CHILD'S SWEATER
Red Heart® Soft®
Variegated - #9954 Bohemian
Orange - #9251 Coral

PONCHO
Red Heart® Super Saver®
Brown - #365 Coffee
Variegated - #928 Earth and Sky

We have made every effort to ensure that these instructions are accurate and complete. We cannot, however, be responsible for human error, typographical mistakes, or variations in individual work.

Production Team: Instructional/Technical Writer - Lois J. Long; Editorial Writer - Susan Frantz Wiles; Senior Graphic Artist - Lora Puls; Graphic Artist - Julian Lyden; Photo Stylist - Lori Wenger; and Photographer - Jason Masters.